M000250076

Dedication

This book is dedicated to my first-born daughter,
Rosie, who has given me love like I've never known.
I hope she will always have the courage and passion
to push through barriers to achieve her dreams.

And to my loving wife, Susie, who always supports
my wild projects and ideas.

www.mascotbooks.com

Baby's First Business Book

©2020 Andrew Dorazio. All Rights Reserved. No part of this publication may be reproduced, stored in a retrieval system or transmitted in any form by any means electronic, mechanical, or photocopying, recording or otherwise without the permission of the author.

For more information, please contact:
Mascot Books
620 Herndon Parkway, Suite 320
Herndon, VA 20170
info@mascotbooks.com

Library of Congress Control Number: 2020900368

CPSIA Code: PRT0720A
ISBN-13: 978-1-64543-414-6

Printed in the United States

Andrew Dorazio

Baby's First Business Book

Illustrated by **Victoria Savanella**

May you be surrounded by accountants to always check your math.

is for...

Accountant

A good accountant is the one to know to help you make your business grow.

B is for...

Bank

A bank is a place to put your cash to ensure that your business continues to last.

May you always have a safe place to keep your money growing.

C

is for...

Cash

Never forget that cash is king.
Invest it wisely from summer to spring.

May you always have cash stashed away for a rainy day.

is for...

Debt

You will never have to worry or fret if you grow your business free of debt.

is for...

Entrepreneur

Owning a business makes you an entrepreneur. Be mindful, though— it is a challenge for sure!

May you always have the grit and perseverance to be an entrepreneur.

F

is for...

Fortune

Your fortune may take
a century to grow, but
be careful, my child—
it's easy to blow.

May you always remember that fortune favors the bold.

Until we live without them,

may we have the strength to break through them.

G is for...

Glass Ceiling

A glass ceiling might not be so easy to see, but punch through it, my child, so at the top you can be.

 is for...

Honesty

She who is honest
knows that it pays to
be truthful in business
for all of her days.

May you always be honest in all of your endeavors.

Investment

is for...

An investment can grow to be big and be tall, but always be wary when its size starts to fall.

May you grow your wealth on your gains,

and your mind on your losses.

is for...

J oint Venture

A joint venture can bring two people together, so you both stay afloat no matter the weather.

May you always choose partners that help make the paddling easier.

is for...

Kindness

No one likes to work with a grouch, so always be kind or your business will slouch.

is for...

Leverage

Leverage can help you lift up the weight, grow your business much faster, and get through the gate.

May you always use leverage wisely.

Marketing

is for...

Marketing will help your business expand, increasing your sales and your money in hand.

May you always know how to reach and impress your market.

May your nest egg always outgrow your dreams.

is for...

Nest Egg

A nest egg is something to protect and to grow, because you may need it sooner than you know.

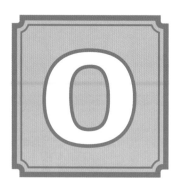

is for...

Organization

Organizing a business can be lots of fun—just don't forget to play in the sun!

May you build an organization that mirrors your values.

May you profit in everything you do.

P

is for...

Profit

Making a profit is the point of the game, but being too greedy could tarnish your name.

Quality

is for...

Always ensure that your products are great, as quality will ensure your business's fate.

May you strive to always do everything with the highest of quality.

is for...

Risk

A risk is something to think of a bunch. Always remember that there is no free lunch.

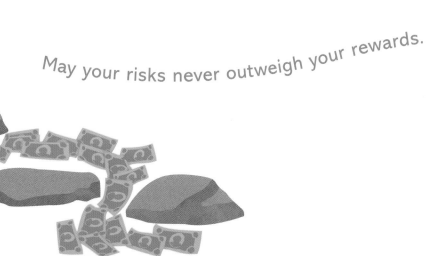

May your risks never outweigh your rewards.

Savings

is for...

Growing your savings can be lots of fun, especially when it allows your business to run.

May you always squirrel some money away for savings.

FINISH

May you never stop searching for sales and spending carefully!

is for...

Thrifty

May you always think it's nifty to run your business lean and thrifty.

May you always be the unicorn in a room full of horses.

U is for...

Unicorn

A unicorn may be
a one in a million,
but that is for
chumps—you are
one in a billion!

Compromise is great, but never on your values.

V is for...

Value

It's easy to value things made of gold; instead try to value things that are bold.

May you always share in the wealth, no matter what it may be.

is for...

Wealth

Wealth can be measured in many a way, but sometimes it's simply the things you share every day.

X is for...

EXpense

An expense can be something that is large or is small, but let them add up and soon your business will fall.

May your expenses

NEVER outgrow your dreams.

Yield

is for...

May your business always grow and give you a yield, similar to farmers who pull from their fields.

May your yields always be fruitful year-round.

is for...

Zero

There is a zero percent chance of giving up on your dreams, as I will always be there to pick you up by your seams.

And may you always know that there is a zero percent chance that I will ever give up on you.

NEVER STOP FOLLOWING YOUR GOALS AND DREAMS

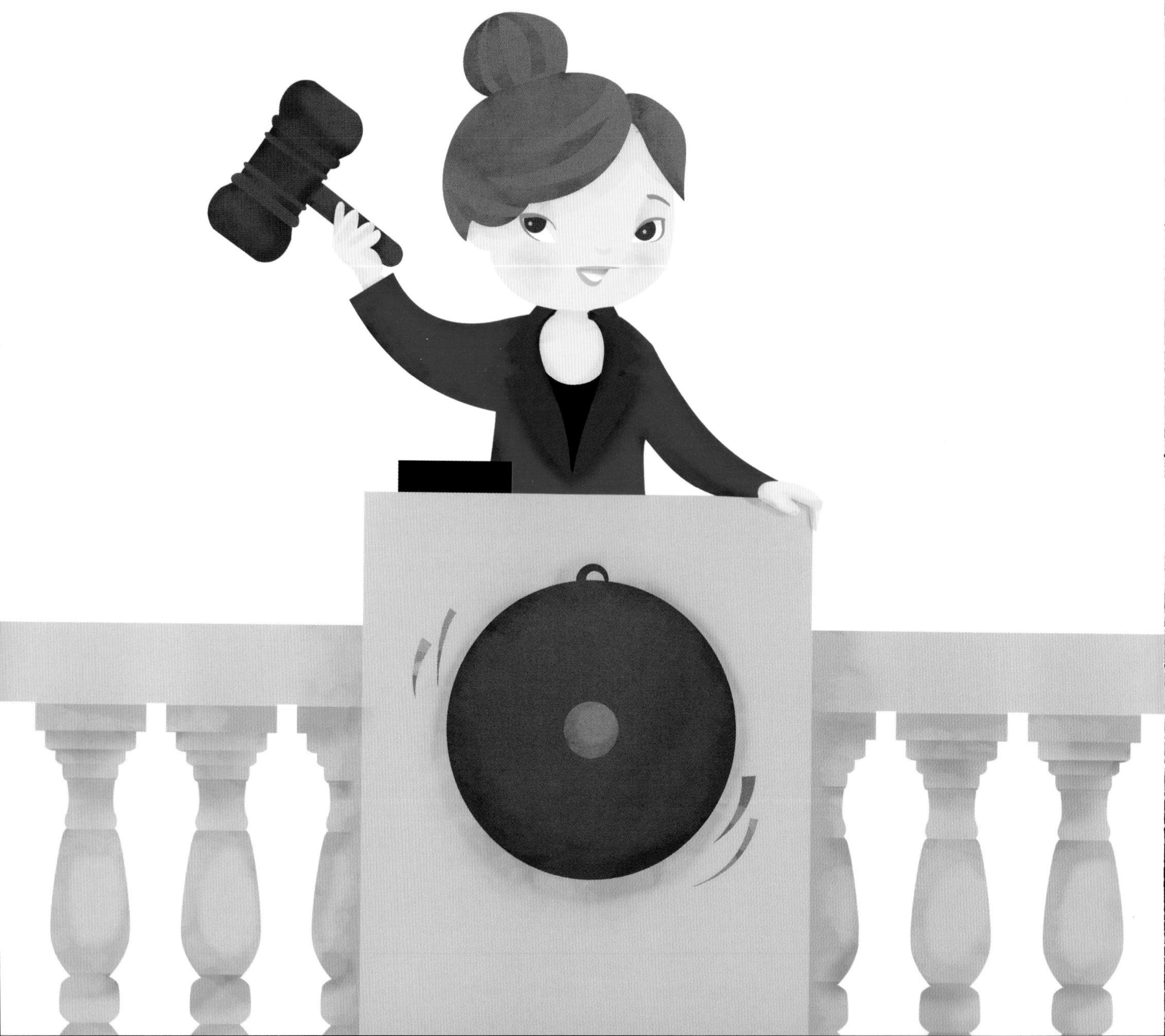

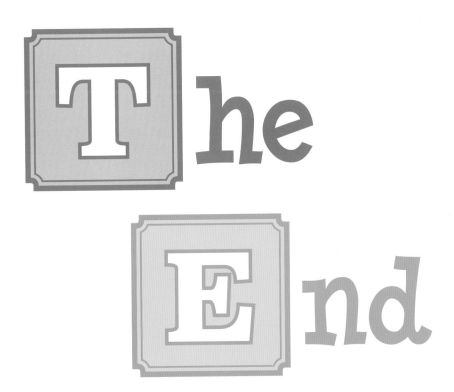

About the Artist

Victoria Savanella is an artist who lives and works in New York's Hudson Valley. She studied fashion and general illustration at the Fashion Institute of Technology. She has illustrated several children's books and contributed artwork to *Weekly Reader* and various children's products. Her artwork is inspired by vintage illustrations. She's very excited to contribute to a book with a positive message for girls!

About the Author

Andrew Dorazio is a former Army officer and current entrepreneur based in Chicago, Illinois. He holds a degree in economics from West Point. His debut children's book, *Baby's First Business Book*, was inspired by the birth of his daughter, Rosie. Andrew and his wife, Susie, love reading to little Rosie, but they quickly realized there were a lack of children's books related to business—especially ones geared towards girls. They decided to write this book to hopefully inspire their daughter and other young girls to be brave enough to start their own business venture one day.